Suicide

Stories of depressive minds

Zartashia Khanum

Suicide is not a cure of any problem, let face the life and live as you want to live. Suicide ideation is actually the absence of normal mental state many factors contribute in formation of this kind of behavior. Here is some solution that will help to eliminate the risk factor of suicide. Live let live

Contents

3

Have you ever thought about suicide? How often you think about suicide? Are you getting separated from your love ones? Do you feel the lack of interest? Ok let's begin to asses a suicidal behavior before starting we need to know more about suicide.

Suicidal behavior is an act that could reason someone to die. Person who has suicidal behavior try different means of self harming for example an excessive dose of drug or intentional accidents. Suicidal behavior by made up out of three particular kind of self annihilative deed, accomplished suicide, half suicide and self injury. Ideas and scheme in connection with suicide are known as suicide ideation. Suicidal behavior is a leading issue for public health precedence. Suicide is still one of the major reasons of death across the world for many decades.

Age group and suicidal behavior

Suicidal tendencies in teenagers (13 to 19) are growing alarmingly, however this age is full of innocence, foolishness as well as naughtiness but along this cherish side this tender age has another side which is quite scary and emotionally unstable. In this age physical, mental, psychological and emotional development of children is booming. Healthy and balanced growth at this particular stage is very important. Teenagers often get angry over trivial things and try to take their own lives. It is very important for parents during this period of education and training take into account the psychological needs of children.

Causes of suicidal behavior

The root of this behavior belongs to early childhood. This behavior may occurred when child get victim of physical and sexual abuse in his early age sometimes it is the negligence of parents or lack of sex education can become the reason for such kind of behavior. Child goes through a mental and emotional trauma that sometimes prompted him to harm himself subsequently.

Use of alcohol, drugs, tobacco increases the risk factor of suicidal behavior. We cannot ignore the mental disorders in this regard; in 90% cases of suicides mental disorders are present, in addition genetics and environment play a vital role in activating this behavior. Furthermore many factors such as social, economical, cultural values contribute to produce suicidal behavior. Overpopulation leads people toward unemployment to much population decreases resources of earning, resulting, in poor society's masses prefer to commit suicide due to hunger.

Domestic violence or abusive relationship is leading problem of the world. Often you heard news regarding Abusive relationship celebrities are also become the victims of it and they become very public. Abuse is not always easily perceived as being jostle, by calling noxious names or abusing. In fact, it can very well be subversive. Sometimes people may find their self confused about the relationship. It seems like they are extremely careful about their relationship. This is the kind of abuse that often creeps up on you as you go more constituted in the relationship. It is known as psychological abuse, we label it as mental or emotional abuse. Psychological abuse is when a person in the relationship tries to control information available to another person with intent to spoof that person's sense of reality or their view of what is acceptable and what is not. Psychological abuse consist on powerful emotionally scheming subject matter and warnings set out to pressurize the victim to abide by with the abuser's choices. All abuse are sever attack on self-esteem. The victim starts feeling helpless and even hopeless. Moreover, most abusers successfully convinced his/her victim that the abuse is only his/her fault. By hook or crook, the victim is responsible for all bad things.

Suicidal behavior amongst LGBT

Studies shows that suicide attempts ratio and suicidal ideation amidst lesbian, gay, bisexual, transgender, queer, and questioning (LGBTQQ) in youth is relatively higher rather than the general population

LGBT teens and young adults have the highest rates of suicide attempts. According to some groups, this is connected to heterocentric societies and institutionalized intense hatred for homosexual in some cases, comprise the use of rights and protections for LGBT people as a political wedge issue like in the contemporary efforts to halt legalizing same-sex marriages.

Depression and use of drug among LGBT people have both been rise notably after new laws that differentiate against gay people are passed.

Bullying behavior

I have seen in many places, societies and different social forums people adopt bullying behavior for LGBT people. Specifically religion and religious people condemn them due to their dogmatic thinking and religion. Let check it out what bible says for homosexuality:

"If a man lies with a male as with a woman, both of them have committed an abomination; they shall surely be put to death; their blood is upon them.' (Chapter 20 verse 13)

What Islam says about homosexuality?

And [We had sent] Lot when he said to his people, "**Do you commit such immorality** as no one has preceded you with from among the world's? (80)**Indeed, you approach men with desire, instead of women. Rather, you are a transgressing people."**(81) Al-Araf 80-81

Religions also adopt bully behavior towards homosexuality.

This bullying behavior has been shown being partly responsible of many suicides, even if not all of the attacks have been specifically addressing sexuality or gender. Since a series of suicides in the early 2000s, directed a great deal of attention on the issues and its hidden causes in an effort to reduce suicides among LGBTQ youth. The Family Acceptance Project's research has demonstrated that "parental acceptance, and even neutrality, with regard to a child's sexual orientation" can bring down the attempted suicide rate. Suicidal ideation and attempts appear to be the same for heterosexual youth as for youth equivalent who have same-sex attractions and behavior but never categorized as being LGBTQ. This correspond with the findings of a large survey of US adults that developed higher ratio of "mood and anxiety disorders, key risk factors for suicidal behavior," are connected to people who recognized as gay, lesbian, and bisexual, rather than sexual behaviors, especially for men Certainly, not every LGBT person attempts suicide – mostly don't make any attempt – but those that do often do so for the reason of the stress of anti-gay stigma, prejudice and harassment. This sort of stress is known as "minority stress" as it is deployed on minority populations. In the LGBT population, more than 75% of people in a community setting reported suffering verbal harassment while one-in-seven reported physical attacks. Internalized homophobia also contributes to LGBT suicide risk.

Family support may also be a key LGBT suicide risk factor. LGB youth who suffered by severe family rejection were more than 8 times allegedly to report having attempted suicide in contrast with peers from families with little or no rejection.

14

LGBT suicide risk elements also comprise previous suicide attempts, present psychiatric conditions and other risk factors that can be exist for anyone.

Psychological trauma

Trauma is a psychological reaction to a harmful or life-threatening occurrence that is outside the range of normal experience and beyond control. Those with histories of trauma may be troubled by thoughts of suicide and some may attempt or complete suicide. Trauma's impact is insidious, pervasive, life changing, and enduring. It most affects those vulnerable because of age or other personal factors. It influences responses to future stressors.

Psychological disorders play a vital role to heighten the risk factor of suicidal behaviour The effects of trauma may include anxiety, depression, hopelessness, despair, anger, hostility, social isolation, impulsiveness, alcohol or substance abuse, self-destructive behavior, humiliation, shame, guilt, lessened self-esteem, a loss of personal beliefs, and feeling ineffective, distrustful, or threatened

Trauma and its side effects are associated with greater suicide risk. A significant number of attempters and completers have a background of trauma. It makes those affected feel less connected or that they are burdens to their families and friends. This generates hopelessness and depression, which may produce a desire to die. Trauma sufferers with a risk of suicide include self-injurers, those making frequent threats or non-fatal attempts, veterans and members of the military, physicians, emergency responders, sexual assault victims, individuals with brain injury, and physically and developmentally disabled persons.

History of suicide

It is difficult to find out the record of very first person who committed suicide; however here is some on the record suicide cases in the history. In general, the pagan world, Roman and Greek, were less anxious behavior towards the concept of suicide. The Council of Arles in 452 stated "if a slave commits suicide no reproach shall fall upon his master." In the Middle Ages, the Church had drawn-out discussions on the edge where the search for martyrdom was suicidal, as in the case of some of the martyrs of Córdoba

There are some precursors of Christian hostility to suicide in ancient Greek thinkers. Pythagoras, for example, was against the act, though more on mathematical than moral grounds, believing that there was only a finite number of souls for use in the world, and that the sudden and unexpected departure of one upset a delicate balance. Aristotle also condemned suicide, though for quite different, far more practical reasons, in that it robbed the community of the services of one of its members. A reading of *Phaedo* suggests that Plato was also against the practice, inasmuch as he allows Socrates to defend the teachings of the Orphics, who believed that the human body was the property of the gods, and thus self-harm was a direct offense against divine law.

The Romans, however, fully approved of what might be termed "patriotic suicide"; death, in other words, as an alternative to dishonor. For the Stoics, a philosophical sect which originated in Greece, death was a guarantee of personal freedom, a way out of an intolerable existence.

In the Middle Ages, the Christian church excommunicated people who attempted suicide and those who died by suicide were buried outside consecrated graveyards. A criminal ordinance issued by Louis XIV of France in 1670 was far more severe in its punishment: the dead person's body was drawn through the streets, face down, and then hung or thrown on a garbage heap. Additionally, all of the person's property was confiscated.

Attitudes towards suicide slowly began to shift during the Renaissance; Thomas More the English humanist, wrote in *Utopia* (1516) that a person afflicted with disease can "free himself from this bitter life...since by death he will put an end not to enjoyment but to torture...it will be a pious and holy action".

In the late 17th and early 18th centuries, loopholes were invented to avoid the damnation that was promised by most Christian doctrine as a penalty of suicide

The secularization of society that began during The Enlightenment questioned traditional religious attitudes toward suicide to eventually form the modern perspective on the issue. David Hume denied that suicide was a crime as it affected no one and was potentially to the advantage of the individual. In his 1777 *Essays on Suicide and the Immortality of the Soul* he rhetorically asked, "Why should I prolong a miserable existence, because of some frivolous advantage which the public may perhaps receive from me?"

Avoid labeling

According to research in a group of 30 students, three students in them present trend of suicides. Often come to the observation that teachers and educational institutions have failed to fulfill their role.

 In some society's teachers labeled students with offensive names like, you are a dull student you can't get success in your life, you are irresponsible, lazy and worthless. Some teachers use to say "I suggest you abandon your education and find some other hobby for yourself. Not only teachers, but our whole society is suffering from this deadly behavior. It's usually happened in the poor or developmental states. This sort of words leaves bad impact on student's minds. Don't label kids by these harsh comments or words like, lazy, dull, and stupid such strong words create frustration in students and cause mental illness. The child begins to like solitude and starts to disconnect from society. Children are beginning to flourish in their inferiority that becomes fatal for them. Suicidal tendencies are effected child's educational process.

Suicidal brain:

According to modern neurological research, human emotions linked to different parts of brain. Frontal lobe play a central role in the neural network for social cognition. Ventral medial frontal regions are responsible for changing behavior. It is connected with amygdale and other limbic structure which belongs to emotions and motivation. Parts of the brain play a central role in suicide because thinking and emotions directly linked with brain. In the case of traumatic brain injury the risk of suicide is increased.

Suicidal behavior grows when and why?

Overall exposure to multiple risk factors

Lack of protective factors

It is important to assess suicidal tendencies following factors should be taken into account; age, gender, nationality, sexual orientation, and easy access to weapons. Suicidal tendencies are also increasing with aging, as I have mentioned above suicidal tendencies are more sever in teenagers. Gender is also a factor affecting property on suicidal behavior. Without any discrimination of race suicidal ideations are found in women, however a women try to take her own life more than twice in her life(CDC 2002); trends of suicide five times more among men of all race (simon et,al,2001) women usually tell someone about their suicide thoughts and ideation. Easy availability of fire arms is also promoting the concepts and thoughts of suicide. If fire arms and pistols are available at home then risk factors increased five times greater. It rarely happens that a person commit suicide suddenly or unexpectedly. Moreover, these people are normally show warning signs which usually can be predicted from their behavior.

To prevent from suicide trends it is important to consider the following factors

Flexibility factors:

Family support and harmony

Parental interest in children

Condemnation of suicidal behavioral at cultural and community level

Moral support to the children by their age fellows and their relationship

Ability to solve problems and social relevance

High self esteem

Mental and physical health care

Children get support by their age fellows and their social relationship.

Risk factors:

Previous suicide attempt

Use of drugs or alcohol

Family background of suicide

Offensive furious attitude

Sexual and physical abuse

Do not accept help for mental health

Cultural and religious beliefs which allow suicide

To be suffering from mental illness especially depression

Hopelessness, helplessness

To hurt himself/ discomfort/ self harm(cutting)

Physical illness

Easy access to lethal and dangerous methods of suicide

Mental and physical health care

Warning signs:

Behavior or habits reveal the intention of suicide

The indirect suicidal thinking

Increases drug use

Person with suicidal behavior expressed their intentions by his words and actions

Often talk about death and suicide

Life is meaningless there is no more purpose of life

Withdrawal from friends and family

Lack of interest in pleasant activities

The change in mood and behavior

Drug use is increasing

Changes in sleep and eating routines

The inability to focus on things and think in illogical manners

Suddenly and unexpectedly cheering

Runaway from home

Changes in sleep and eating routines

The inability to focus on things and fail to think logical

Suddenly and unexpectedly cheering

Run away from away

Acting impulsively

Poor performance in school or at work

Unreasonable shame and guilt feelings

Cases of suicides and suicidal ideations

My client who witnessed suicide told me

" I had seen three suicide cases and three cases are entirely different from each other. When I was in 5th grade my class mate committed suicide because he did not get any position in the class he was so afraid that his parents would punish him. He shot in his head by his father's gun.

2nd suicide case occurred to this year (2016) the person who committed suicide is my cousin. He was a businessman he borrowed money for their business but he failed to pay his debt and shot himself.

And the third of our university lecturer who killed himself for the sake of love.

One of my clients who has suicide ideation. He is suffering by dysthymia and border line personality disorder. He used to tell me his story. I have parents but I spent a life like orphans (both emotionally and financially). I was very sensitive and had low tolerance level of stress. I did run away from home multiple times. Tried to commit suicide at least 3 times in my early twenties I met someone and my life was changed. I got best friend in form her and an understanding and appreciating mother in form of her mother. Haven't thought about it ever since. Abandoning religion also helped to make my thought process clearer. I was very lucky I guess. However not everyone is. This typical shit we are given that we should not disrespect our parents no matter what is so out dated. I believe respect is earned. I have none for my parents and I intend to abandon them after marriage.

Famous Celebrities suicides

Jeff Alm

Committed Suicide: 1993

Jeff Alm was an American footballer who played for National Football League. According to report that Alm had a 14 or over blood alcohol-level. Alm was also using the prescript barbiturate, fiorinal, generally recommended for Tension Headache.

The Von Erich Family

The Von Erich family is a professional wrestling family

Michael, Chris, and Kerry all committed suicide in 1987, 1991, and
1993 resultantly. Mike died by taking an overdose of Placadyl. Chris
killed himself with a 9mm pistol at his parents' house which located in East Texas.
Kerry shot himself in the chest back of his father's home on.

Del Shannon

**Committed
Suicide: 1990**

Del Shannon was an American rock and roll singer-songwriter who had a No.
1 hit single with Runaway in 1961.

 He suffered from extreme
depression and alcoholism throughout his life and committed suicide on
February 8, 1990, with a 22 caliber rifle.

Brad Delp

Committed Suicide: 2007

Brad Delp was an American musician. On March 9, 2007,
Delp was found dead in his home in Atkinson. The cause of death was carbon monoxide poisoning.

Robert Enke

Committed Suicide: 2009

His widow Teresa revealed that her husband had been suffering from depression and was treated by a psychiatrist.

Dipendra of Nepal

Committed Suicide: 2001

Dipendra Bir Bikram Shah was a member of the Nepalese Royal Family,

who briefly became King of Nepal from June 1 to
June 4, 2001

According to reports, Dipendra had been drinking
heavily and had
"misbehaved" with a guest, which resulted in his
father, King Birendra, telling
his son to leave the party. The drunken Dipendra
was taken to his room by
his brother Prince Nirajan and cousin Prince
Paras. One hour later, he
allegedly returned to the party armed with an
MP5K and an M16 and began
executing the guests. After killing ten people he
shot himself in the head and
died three days later.

Alberto Santos Dumont

Committed Suicide: 1932

Alberto Santos Dumont was an early pioneer of aviation. Alberto Santos Dumont became seriously ill and depressed over his multiple sclerosis and the use of aircraft in warfare.

Kurt Cobain

Committed Suicide: 1994

Kurt Cobain was an American songwriter and musician, best known as the
lead singer and guitarist of the rock band Nirvana. Cobain struggled with heroin addiction, illness and depression, his fame and public image, as well as the professional and
lifelong personal pressures surrounding himself

and his wife, musician
Courtney Love.

On April 8, 1994, Cobain was found dead at his
home in Seattle, the victim
of what was officially ruled a suicide by a self-
inflicted shotgun wound to the
head.

Robin Williams

He was exceptionally talented actor (comedian) of Hollywood. Robin Williams was suffering of each of two depression or manic depressive illness. Williams was also combat with addiction and mental illness. Hollywood star Robin Williams took his own life by hanging himself by his belt at his bed room.

Chris Benoit 1967

Chris Benoit was brilliant wrestling super star. On June 22 he murdered his wife and son, and afterwards hanged himself on June 24, 2007. According to report depression and brain damage accumulated from various injuries are predisposed subsidize aspects dominant to Benoit's suicide and murdered.

Psychological disorders

Drug abuse

Manic depression

Panic attacks

Schizophrenia

Borderline personality disorders

Narcissistic personality disorder

How to deal with suicidal behavior and ideation

Seemingly it is almost impossible to deal suicidal behavior and suicide in many suicide cases the person usually diagnosed of chronic psychological disorders especially major depression and drug abuse. Suicidal ideation is more common rather than suicide attempts or accomplished suicide. But my point was how someone deal this kind of behavior. If you are suffering by these traumatic thoughts then try to engage yourself in productive or healthy activities. Instead of over thinking on your issues sensitively try to analyze your issue in realistic or sensible manners after few times you realized your suicide ideation does not consist on sound grounds suddenly you feel it's all stupid thought which you were going to die for. Another tact to get rid of these thoughts, indulge yourself in any useful and refresher hobby like gardening or any as you like. Books reading, especially some light stuff that changes your mood positively. Music listening, Music releases a chemical in the brain that has a key role in setting good moods, a study has suggested.

The study, reported in **Nature Neuroscience**, found that the chemical was released at moments of peak enjoyment. When you are in your blues go for music; don't go for sad music in depression listen fast or rock music, it brings a sudden pleasant change in your mood. In depressive mood don't let yourself alone, go to the public places or meet your friends or do some parties it relax your mind from painful situations. Brain is habit making machine try to train your brain to come out successfully from any difficult situation.

Suicide rates across the world

800,000 and over people die across the world due to suicide every year and there are a lot more cases of people who attempt suicide. Therefore, millions of people are influenced or experience suicide misfortune every year. Suicide betides far and wide the lifespan and was the leading cause of death among 13-29 year olds globally in 2012.

You can't write about stuff you don't know about. You have to live it. You have to roll up your sleeves and get your hands dirty. Live life to be a good songwriter.

Dierks Bentle

47

www.ingramcontent.com/pod-product-compliance
Lightning Source LLC
Chambersburg PA
CBHW070842310526
45793CB00011B/504